W9-CDO-134

SNAPSHOTS IN HISTORY

THE
JAPANESE AMERICAN
INTERNMENT

Civil Liberties Denied

by Michael Burgan

SNAPSHOTS I

THE JAPANESE AMERICAN INTERNMENT

Civil Liberties Denied

by Michael Burgan

Content Adviser: Allan W. Austin, Ph.D.,
Assistant Professor of History, College Misericordia

Reading Adviser: Katie Van Sluys, Ph.D.,
School of Education, DePaul University

Compass Point Books ◈ Minneapolis, Minnesota

THE JAPANESE AMERICAN INTERNMENT

COMPASS POINT BOOKS

3109 West 50th Street, #115
Minneapolis, MN 55410

Visit Compass Point Books on the Internet at
www.compasspointbooks.com
or e-mail your request to
custserv@compasspointbooks.com

For Compass Point Books
Jennifer VanVoorst, Jaime Martens, XNR Productions, Inc.,
Catherine Neitge, Keith Griffin, and Carol Jones

Produced by White-Thomson Publishing Ltd.

For White-Thomson Publishing
Stephen White-Thomson, Susan Crean, Amy Sparks,
Tinstar Design Ltd., Allan W. Austin, Peggy Bresnick Kendler,
Will Hare, and Timothy Griffin

Library of Congress Cataloging-in-Publication Data
Burgan, Michael.
  The Japanese American Internment : civil liberties denied / by
Michael Burgan.
      p. cm. — (Snapshots in history)
  Includes bibliographical references and index.
  ISBN-13: 978-0-7565-2453-1 (library binding)
  ISBN-10: 0-7565-2453-9 (library binding)
  ISBN-13: 978-0-7565-3181-2 (paperback)
  ISBN-10: 0-7565-3181-0 (paperback)
1. Japanese Americans—Evacuation and relocation, 1942–1945—
Juvenile literature. 2. World War, 1939–1945—Japanese Americans—
Juvenile literature. 3. Japanese—United States—History—Juvenile
literature. I. Title. II. Series.
  D769.8.A6B84 2006
  940.53'1773—dc22   2006027080

NOTICE
Headquarters
Western Defense Command
and Fourth Army
Civilian Exclusion Order No. 1
Western Defense Command and Fourth Army
Wartime Civil Control Administration
INSTRUCTIONS TO ALL
JAPANESE
Living on Bainbridge Island
MP
57

CONTENTS

Leaving Home

In the early months of 1942, 20-year-old Yoshiko Uchida and her family joined tens of thousands of Japanese Americans in a sad departure. The Uchidas, who lived in Berkeley, California, loaded a truck with beds and other items to place in storage. They sold their refrigerator, vacuum cleaner, and other household goods to their neighbors. Then Yoshiko and her family jammed suitcases and bags with clothes and other personal items. They brought only the essentials needed in their new home, and they said goodbye to their comfortable three-bedroom house with a neat yard and fruit trees.

The Uchidas first reported to a local church that served as what the U.S. government called a Civil Control Station. Yoshiko later wrote about what she saw at the church: "Armed guards [were] standing at each doorway, their bayonets mounted and ready."

Although she knew what was going on, it wasn't until that moment that she really felt the horror of what was happening to her and her family. The U.S. government considered them a threat and would not let them live their lives as they once had.

In a short time, Yoshiko and other Japanese Americans boarded a bus that took them to an assembly center. Within a few months, they would move again to what the U.S. government called relocation centers. Others called them internment or concentration camps. Regardless of their name, Yoshiko and the other internees knew their freedom was gone.

U.S. soldiers searched the belongings of Japanese Americans before they entered the Santa Anita reception center in Los Angeles, California

On December 7, 1941, several months before the relocation of the Uchida family, Japan had launched a surprise attack on the U.S. naval base at Pearl Harbor, Hawaii. At that time, agents from the Federal Bureau of Investigation arrested Yoshiko Uchida's father in California, where he was living with his family.

U.S. President Franklin D. Roosevelt and his advisers feared that some Japanese Americans who were aliens, or non-U.S. citizens, might spy for Japan or otherwise harm the American war effort. Uchida was one of several thousand Japanese American aliens who were arrested soon after the incident at Pearl Harbor. That left Yoshiko, her sister, and their mother to go alone to the assembly center.

ALIENS AND CITIZENS

Immigrants from Japan, or any other country, to the United States are called aliens. After living in the country for five years, aliens who entered the country legally can apply for U.S. citizenship. This process is called naturalization, and the aliens are then known as naturalized citizens. However, at the time of internment, first-generation Japanese Americans were barred by law from naturalization. The children of either legal or illegal aliens who are born in the United States automatically become U.S. citizens. The Japanese had special names for immigrant aliens and citizens:

Born in Japan (alien)	Issei
Born in the United States (U.S. citizen)	Nisei
U.S. citizen educated in Japan	Kibei

After 1941, Japanese men were thought to be dangerous, and many were arrested in Hawaii and several Western states. Their names were taken from lists created by the U.S. government before the Pearl Harbor attack.

The Uchidas' assembly center was Tanforan, a racetrack in San Bruno, California. Yoshiko and many others found themselves living in old horse stalls. The government had spread a chemical called lye to mask the smell of the animals that had once lived there, but the lye could not hide the fact that the stalls had been used as the animals' bathroom.

11

Even the youngest Japanese Americans brought only what they could carry as they left for the relocation centers.

After inspecting what was to be her new home, Yoshiko went to the dining hall. The first meal served to her at the camp was canned sausage, a boiled potato, and a slice of bread with no butter. Yoshiko recalled:

> *Once we got into the gloomy, cavernous mess hall, I saw hundreds of people eating at wooden picnic tables, while those who had already eaten were shuffling aimlessly over the wet cement floor. We tried to eat,*

*but the food would not go down. We decided
it would be better to go back to our barracks
than to linger in the depressing confusion
of the mess hall. Once back in our stall, we
found it no less depressing, for there was only
a single electric light bulb dangling from the
ceiling, and a one-inch crevice at the top of
the north wall admitted a steady draft of the
cold night air. We sat huddled in our cots,
bundled in our coats, too cold and miserable
even to talk.*

The assembly center was just a temporary stop
for the Uchidas. The government kept the Japanese
Americans in the centers until the relocation centers
were completed. The Uchidas stayed at Tanforan for
just over three months. They were then transfered
to Topaz, a camp in Utah. By this time, Mr. Uchida
had been allowed to join his family.

Once they reached the relocation centers,
Yoshiko and the others found conditions were
only a little better. Although the meals were more
plentiful and the rooms did not smell, the internees
were forced to live behind barbed wire. Armed men
stood guard, making sure they did not escape. At
Topaz, dust swirled everywhere, and at night ice
formed on the kettle of water the family kept in
their room. Yoshiko and her family often suffered
from colds and upset stomachs as they tried to
adjust to a climate and diet different from what
they had known at home. Yoshiko was lucky. She
was allowed to leave Topaz in the spring of 1943 to
work at a college in Massachusetts. Her sister also

left for school. Their parents, however, remained behind, and some internees would live behind the barbed wire throughout the war, which finally ended in 1945.

Many of the people who supported the creation of the camps genuinely feared a Japanese invasion of the United States. The Japanese attack on Pearl Harbor had brought the United States into World War II. Many Americans believed the

Most Americans of Japanese descent were sent to internment camps during World War II.

Japanese would strike again in Hawaii, or perhaps even attack the West Coast of the United States. At the time, most Japanese Americans lived in the West, particularly in California, Oregon, and Washington. Some U.S. leaders worried that the Japanese Americans—even those who were U.S. citizens—would be disloyal to the United States. Sending them to the camps where their actions could be controlled seemed the only way to guarantee the security of the country.

The drive to detain Japanese Americans was also fueled by racism. Fear and hatred of the Japanese in the United States had first emerged long before World War II. Some lawmakers and newspaper publishers wrongly believed the Japanese people were warlike and deceitful by nature. One California member of Congress noted what he called "the treacherous way they do things."

The Uchidas were among nearly 120,000 Japanese Americans who went to the camps during World War II. More than half of them, such as Yoshiko and her sister, were U.S. citizens. Most historians agree that these citizens were unfairly denied their civil rights as outlined in the U.S. Constitution.

The last Japanese Americans left the camps in 1946, more than six months after World War II ended. The internment had changed their lives and raised questions about the proper actions to take during wartime—questions still debated today. ◣

Before Pearl Harbor

Chapter

2

In 1869, a group of approximately 20 Japanese immigrants became the first Japanese people to settle in the United States. With the help of a Dutch businessman, they went to Gold Hill, California, to raise crops and produce silk. A shortage of water and money, however, led to the failure of the Gold Hill settlement. Within a year or so, the country's first Japanese immigrants had scattered around California.

Starting in the 1890s, the number of Japanese immigrants coming to the United States rose. Approximately 27,000 came to the country between 1891 and 1900, and that number increased to almost 130,000 the next decade. More than 75 percent of the newcomers went to California, Oregon, and Washington, with California drawing the most.

Seattle, Washington, was home to many successful Japanese American business owners, such as Tsnta Kawa.

17

At first, the immigrants took a variety of jobs, such as mining, building railroads, and canning food. Over time, most turned to agriculture, particularly in California. After first working for American farmers, many Japanese saved money and bought their own land. With hard work, they created some of the most successful farms in the state. Other Japanese immigrants opened successful businesses.

At the same time as the arrival of the first Japanese immigrants in California, about 150 Japanese were brought to Hawaii to work in the sugar cane fields. Hawaii was then an independent kingdom, which became a U.S. territory in 1898. But even before then, U.S. companies dominated Hawaii's economy, owning the sugar cane fields and other businesses there.

The increasing number of Japanese immigrants— and their growing success—upset some people in the western United States. The Pacific Coast had already gone through a period of intense racism against another group of people from Asia—the

THE POTATO KING

One of the Japanese immigrants who succeeded in California farming was Kinji Ushijima. In 1889, the 26-year-old settled in California, and unlike many Japanese immigrants, Ushijima arrived with some money. He bought swampland outside Sacramento. Ushijima drained the land and began to raise potatoes. By 1913, he had changed his name to George Shima and become the most famous Japanese American in the country. His farming empire had expanded to 28,000 acres (11,200 hectares), he employed about 500 people, and he became known as the Potato King. When he died in 1926, his fortune was worth an estimated $15 million.

Many Japanese people who emigrated to Hawaii in the early 1900s worked in sugar cane fields there.

Chinese. Many Chinese immigrants had come to the United States during the 1850s, lured by the California Gold Rush. Others came to work in mines and build railroads.

19

Racism against the Chinese led the U.S. government to pass the Chinese Exclusion Act of 1882. This was the first law designed to keep out immigrants from one particular country. By 1900, some Americans were associating the Japanese with the Chinese. Both were Asian. Both came from non-Christian countries that did not have democratic governments, as the United States did. In 1900, James D. Phelan, the mayor of San Francisco, said of the Japanese: "They are not the stuff of which American citizens can be made."

Such anti-Japanese feelings sometimes led to racist acts. In 1906, officials in San Francisco began forcing all Japanese American students into separate schools, and mobs sometimes attacked Japanese workers. Japan was by that time a powerful nation, and it did not like to see people of Japanese descent treated badly in other countries. Japanese officials asked President Theodore Roosevelt to investigate the situation in California. Roosevelt worried that white mobs in San Francisco might "perform acts of lawless violence [against the Japanese] that would plunge us into war."

By 1907, Roosevelt had worked out a deal with Japan. The Japanese government agreed to stop issuing passports to workers hoping to go to the United States. The Japanese government supported the integration of Japanese Americans into U.S. schools, so in return, Roosevelt persuaded San Francisco officials to allow Japanese students to attend white schools. He also promised Japan that the United States would not pass a law that prevented all Japanese citizens from coming to the United States. The deal between the United States and Japan was called the Gentlemen's Agreement. As Roosevelt hoped, the agreement lessened the tension in U.S.-Japanese relations. It also reduced the number of Japanese immigrants coming to the United States.

The Gentlemen's Agreement, however, did not put an end to anti-Japanese sentiment in California. Caucasian farmers resented the success of the Japanese Americans. Although they owned just 1 percent of the farmland in the state, Japanese Americans produced 10 percent of the crops grown there. By 1913, California lawmakers took action against Japanese Americans. The Alien Land Law targeted the Issei, the Japanese who had come directly from Japan, rather than the Nisei, who were born in the United States. The law drew on another U.S. law that said Asian immigrants could not become naturalized U.S. citizens. The 1913 California law said "aliens ineligible for citizenship" could not own land, which clearly meant the Issei. In 1916, a Japanese businessman named Takao Ozawa

---

PICTURE BRIDES

Under the Gentlemen's Agreement, Japanese immigrants already in the United States could bring family members over. Some of the Japanese men in the United States began marrying women still living in Japan, since there were so few Japanese women in the United States. Often they had never met these women but had simply received a picture of them from friends or families. The wedding ceremonies were held in Japan, with another man acting as a substitute for the husband who was in the United States. These new wives were called picture brides, and they soon joined their husbands in the United States.

challenged the law barring the naturalization of Japanese aliens, but in 1922, the U.S. Supreme Court upheld the ban.

Although they had limited rights, Japanese immigrants in the early 1900s quickly adapted to the American way of life.

Other Western states passed land laws similar to California's. Still, some Issei were able to purchase

22

or hold land in the name of their Nisei children. Since the Nisei were born in the United States, they were automatically U.S. citizens. A second California law passed in 1920 made it harder for the Issei to use this loophole and own land through their children. Aliens could no longer control land owned by their children, and land purchased by Nisei with their parents' money could be taken away by the state.

In 1924, Congress passed a new law restricting immigration. Almost all immigration from Japan ended. The Japanese American presence on the Pacific Coast continued to grow, however, as young couples started families. By 1930, nearly 140,000 Japanese lived in the United States, and almost nine out of 10 of them lived on the West Coast. As a group, the Japanese continued to do well in agriculture, and some were also successful running small stores and other businesses.

In 1931, Japan caught the world's attention with its invasion of Manchuria, a region of China. By the next year, it had established a "puppet" government there—Chinese officials ran the government, but they followed orders sent from Japan.

In March 1933, Franklin D. Roosevelt became president of the United States. His family had once had strong business ties with China, and Roosevelt worried about further Japanese advances there. He also saw Japan as an American rival for dominance of the Pacific Ocean. On entering the White House, Joseph Grew, the U.S. ambassador to Japan, told Roosevelt, "The Japanese fighting forces consider the United States as their potential enemy."

In addition to Hawaii, the United States controlled the Philippines and several small Pacific islands and sought to expand its trade in the Far East. Japan, meanwhile, wanted to increase its own influence in the region, which led its leaders to believe they would one day have to battle the United States. Roosevelt said that the thirst for war was "in the blood" of Japan's leaders.

Japanese troops used both horses and motorized vehicles as they enforced Japan's control over Manchuria.

In 1934, Roosevelt asked for a study of possible Japanese espionage on the West Coast. For the rest of the decade, government agents continued to look for suspicious activity among Japanese Americans or Japanese aliens living in the United States. The fear of Japanese spying grew after 1939. That September, World War II began in Europe with Germany's invasion of Poland. Japan had already taken over more of China and soon became allies with Germany. Japanese troops seemed ready to carry out further attacks, especially against colonies owned by Great Britain, the major ally of the United States.

At first, most Americans wanted to stay out of World War II. By 1940, however, Roosevelt knew the country had to prepare for war against both Germany and Japan. Over the next year, relations between Japan and the United States worsened. The United States sent aid to China for its ongoing war against the Japanese. President Roosevelt also tried to weaken Japan by limiting the goods it could buy from U.S. companies. These actions angered the Japanese government. War between the United States and Japan drew even closer, and Japanese Americans would soon be caught in the middle. ◣

Wartime Fears

Chapter

3

In the fall of 1941, American and Japanese diplomats were still talking to each other. The U.S. government, however, had broken the secret code Japan used when sending messages to its diplomats in the United States. President Roosevelt soon learned that the Japanese were actively preparing to fight.

Roosevelt and his advisers believed that the Japanese would launch a surprise attack on U.S. forces in the Philippines. Japan might also strike at British bases in Asia, forcing the Americans to help their ally. A distant possibility was an attack on Hawaii, but the naval officers there did not expect that to happen. Little did they know that the attack on Pearl Harbor in December 1941 would lead the United States into war against Japan.

President Roosevelt (middle) and his military aides asked Congress for a declaration of war against Japan on December 8, 1941.

Before the attack on Pearl Harbor even took place, President Roosevelt had ordered his aides to conduct a new study on the loyalty of Japanese Americans. Would they support Japan if it launched a surprise attack? Referring to the Nisei, the second-generation Japanese Americans, the report said:

> *We do not want to throw a lot of American citizens into a concentration camp, of course, and especially as the almost unanimous verdict is that in the case of war they will be very, very quiet. ... Because in addition to being quite contented with the American way of life, they know they are "in a spot."*

The report said that if war came, the Japanese Americans would not want to anger U.S. leaders in any way. Instead, they would try hard to prove their loyalty and not further anger the racists who disliked them. Yet the report also said some Japanese Americans might spy for Japan or carry out sabotage.

As Roosevelt and his advisers had anticipated, the Japanese did indeed attack—but not where they had expected. In the early morning hours of Sunday, December 7, 1941, Japanese planes filled the sky over Hawaii. The Japanese surprised the Americans by attacking the part of the U.S. Navy based at Pearl Harbor. For two hours, the Japanese attacked U.S. ships docked in the harbor. Japanese forces also destroyed planes on the ground. When the smoke lifted, 21 U.S. ships had either sunk or been damaged, and more than 3,500 Americans had been killed or wounded. Daniel Inouye, who later became a U.S. senator, was a Japanese American teenager living in Hawaii on the island of Oahu, where Pearl Harbor was located. Inouye later remembered thinking:

> *What would become of the [Japanese Americans] ... suddenly rendered so vulnerable and helpless by this monstrous betrayal at the hands of [Japan]? ... I, too, had been betrayed, and all of my family.*

The Japanese attack on Pearl Harbor sank or damaged eight U.S. battleships, the most powerful ships in the Navy's fleet.

After Japan's attack, the United States declared war on Japan, and suspicion of Japanese Americans soared. In Hawaii, the government ordered martial law, meaning that the military took control of the local police and government. They did this in order to lower the risk of sabotage and espionage by disloyal Japanese Americans. Immediately after the bombing, Roosevelt approved the arrest of 2,000 Issei living in the United States. The government had already determined that they posed possible threats to the United States because of their presumed loyalty to Japan.

A few journalists and political leaders on the West Coast, however, called for Roosevelt to put Japanese Americans in concentration camps. Henry Morgenthau, one of Roosevelt's advisers, dismissed the idea. He said the government should not be "suddenly mopping up 150,000 Japanese and putting them behind barbed wire." But as the days and weeks went on, the call for action against the Japanese Americans grew.

Rumors added to the fear of Japanese Americans. Newspapers reported that

ENEMY ALIENS

After the attack on Pearl Harbor, the Issei became known as enemy aliens, since they were born in a country at war with the United States. In the days after the attack, Germany and Italy also declared war on the United States. Nearly 1 million citizens from those two nations living in the United States were now enemy aliens as well. Like the Japanese, some of them were considered threats to U.S. security and were forced to move, but only about 15,000 were sent to internment camps. Unlike the Japanese, the Italians and Germans were Caucasians like most Americans, and so they did not face the same kind of prejudice the Japanese did.

Japanese planes were seen flying over the West Coast, and civilian boats were flashing messages to Japanese warships at sea. Even some military officers spread rumors, warning that the Japanese would soon attack the mainland United States. The rumors, however, were all false, as were reports that Japanese Americans in Hawaii had acted as spies for Japan.

In 1941, California was still the home of the largest population of Japanese Americans. Fear and hatred of the Japanese was strongest there. After the war began, California was at the heart of what the government called the Western Defense Command. This military organization was supposed to protect the entire West Coast from enemy attack. Its head was General John DeWitt. He, like many other

General John DeWitt was the military head of the Western Defense Command in California.

Americans on the West Coast, spoke openly about Japanese Americans in racist terms. DeWitt used a common slur of the time against the Japanese when he said, "A Jap's a Jap, I don't want any of them."

Before the end of December 1941, General DeWitt called for moving all Issei over the age of 14 far from the West Coast. The Issei were enemy aliens—non-U.S. citizens born in a country now at war with the United States. A government order limited how much money enemy aliens could take out of their bank accounts. First lady Eleanor Roosevelt saw how hard this restriction made it for Issei families to live. Through her efforts, the government eventually let the Issei take out $100 each month from their accounts.

At this time, DeWitt did not think it was legal to send the Nisei to any kind of internment camp.

WHAT KIND OF CAMP?

Internment or concentration camps were first used at the end of the 1800s during wars fought in Cuba and South Africa. Officials believed it would be easier to control civilians they thought might be possible troublemakers if all of them were concentrated in one spot. In 1936, when President Roosevelt first talked about the possibility of relocating Japanese Americans, he used the term concentration camp. By 1942, however, the preferred term was relocation center. Germany, one of the country's enemies in World War II, had built concentration camps for Jews and other people it thought did not deserve full legal rights. The U.S. government did not want people to compare the camps for the Japanese Americans with the camps set up by the Germans.

Others in the government, however, disagreed. Leland Ford, a member of the U.S. House of Representatives from California, said, "All Japanese, whether citizen or not ... [should be] placed in inland concentration camps."

Slowly, more lawmakers in the West began to accept this idea. Some farmers supported the idea of forcing the Japanese from their homes. They saw internment as their chance to gain control of land that the Japanese owned.

President Roosevelt knew about the growing debate over what to do with Japanese Americans. Still, he had little time to focus on it. He was more concerned with preparing the country to fight against both Japan and its European allies, Germany and Italy. Government lawyers, military officers, and lawmakers largely shaped the plans for dealing with the Japanese in the United States.

At first, Roosevelt listened to aides and government officials who said that Japanese Americans would mostly remain loyal. Yet the president refused to make a public statement saying that the Nisei, and most Issei, were not a danger to the country. Those words might have calmed some of the growing fears that Japanese Americans were, or would soon be, disloyal to the United States.

Through January 1942, racist statements against the Japanese Americans continued. So did the calls for interning all Issei as well as Nisei on the mainland. Secretary of the Navy Frank Knox and other officials were also worried about the Japanese Americans living in the U.S. territory of Hawaii and called for locking them up as well, either on one of Hawaii's islands or on the mainland. Military officials in Hawaii, however, opposed the plan. Japanese, both Issei and Nisei, made up about one-third of Hawaii's population. They were needed to help rebuild Pearl Harbor and perform other important jobs. Out of about 150,000 Japanese in Hawaii, only about 1,500 were considered especially dangerous, and they were arrested. Many of them were involved in groups with direct ties to Japan. The rest remained free.

Back in California, General DeWitt was busy preparing to remove Issei from areas near military bases or defense plants in the state. He told another general that he expected "a violent outburst of coordinated and controlled sabotage" by Japanese Americans. To DeWitt, the fact that this violence had not happened merely showed how well Japan controlled its agents in the United States. He believed the disloyal Japanese Americans were simply waiting for their orders to strike. He

THE JAPANESE IN CANADA

While the U.S. government was debating what to do with the Issei and Nisei, Canada took steps against its Japanese residents. As in the United States, most people of Japanese descent in Canada lived on the West Coast. On January 14, 1942, the Canadian government began making plans to intern male enemy aliens between the ages of 18 and 45. Eventually, whole families were sent to what the government called protective areas. In the end, about 21,000 Japanese Canadians were sent to the camps. More than half were citizens. As in the United States, racism and fear fueled the decision to force the Japanese from their homes.

was also beginning to accept the argument that all Japanese Americans should be interned. Other important officials in the government also shared that view.

By mid-February 1942, Japan had won several major victories in the Pacific. Rumors of Japanese attacks on the United States remained common, and people still worried about the loyalty of Japanese Americans. Under these conditions, U.S. officials who favored internment finally persuaded President Roosevelt to take steps in that direction. On February 19, 1942, Roosevelt issued Executive Order 9066. This presidential order gave the military the power to list areas of the country "from which any or all persons may be excluded."

Roosevelt did not mention any particular group of people, but the military and civilian officials who would carry out the plan knew that Japanese Americans were the target of the order.

General DeWitt and others believed there was no way to tell a disloyal Japanese American from a patriotic one. The only way to keep the country safe was to lock up all of them. The president agreed, even though many people in his government continued to claim that the Issei and Nisei did not pose a threat to U.S. security. The pressure to take action against the Japanese Americans was too much for Roosevelt to ignore. ◣

Into the Camps

Chapter

4

Before President Roosevelt issued Executive Order 9066, several thousand Japanese Americans took action of their own. After Pearl Harbor, these Japanese Americans left the West Coast and moved farther inland. Perhaps there, they believed, they could find acceptance. Instead, some found armed civilians who would not let them enter their states. A government report noted that some of the Japanese Americans were thrown into jail for no reason, and "many were greeted by 'No Japs Wanted' signs on the main streets of interior communities."

Most of the Japanese Americans who headed east soon returned to the West Coast, where at least they had friends and family. Soon all these Japanese Americans would be swept up in the relocation process.

Starting in March 1942, General DeWitt released to the news media his first plans for relocating the Japanese Americans. They would be forced out of an area called the Prohibited Zone, which ran the entire length of the Pacific Coast and along part of the border with Mexico. Farther inland, he created the Restricted Zone, where Japanese Americans would have limited freedom to work and live. To help DeWitt with his plan, Congress made it a crime for anyone to refuse to leave a military exclusion area, such as the Prohibited Zone.

Soon signs began appearing on telephone poles and in store windows in Japanese neighborhoods across California. They also went up in parts of Oregon, Washington, and Arizona. The signs told Japanese Americans to go to assembly centers.

A Seattle department store window reflected the anti-Japanese feelings after Pearl Harbor. The store's display used a cartoon image typical of the time.

If they refused to go voluntarily, they would be removed by force. They could only bring with them what they could carry. Many families held huge yard sales to sell the items they could not bring. Others sent their belongings to warehouses, where the government said it would store the goods. Family pets had to be left with friends and neighbors.

At the end of March, the first evacuation took place on Bainbridge Island, Washington. It was quickly followed by evacuations in California. Most of the evacuees volunteered to go. The military did not have to use force, even though it was allowed. Many Japanese American leaders had said the Issei and Nisei should cooperate with the government. Going voluntarily would show their loyalty to the United States.

A military police officer nailed up the first posters announcing the evacuation of Japanese Americans in Bainbridge Island, Washington.

A Nisei group called the Japanese American Citizens League (JACL) led the effort to persuade the Japanese Americans to go along with the relocation. Mike Masaoka, the leader of the JACL, told a newspaper in Los Angeles:

> *We want to convince them that it will be patriotic to make this sacrifice, and a sacrifice it will be. We seek to make our people look at this movement as a sort of adventure, such as our fathers and mothers undertook when they came to this country.*

In 1940, Masaoka wrote the Japanese American Creed, which outlined the beliefs of the JACL and its members. The next year, he had the creed printed in the *Congressional Record*, the official journal of Congress. It reads, in part:

> *I am proud that I am an American citizen of Japanese ancestry, for my very background makes me appreciate more fully the wonderful advantages of this nation. I believe in her institutions, ideals and traditions; I glory in her heritage; I boast of her history; I trust in her future. She has granted me liberties and opportunities such as no individual enjoys in this world today.*

> *Although some individuals may discriminate against me I shall never become bitter or lose faith, for I know such persons are not representative of the majority of the American people.*

Mike Masaoka was a teacher in Utah before joining the JACL. He later served as a private in the Army after Nisei were allowed to volunteer.

Only a few Japanese Americans spoke out against relocation. One of them was James Omura, a Nisei who lived in California. In February 1942, he protested the relocation to members of Congress. Before the relocation began in California, Omura had moved to Denver, Colorado. Not many Japanese Americans lived there, and the city was far from the coast, where a Japanese invasion was most likely. For these reasons, Japanese Americans in this area were not considered a threat and forced into camps. Omura, a journalist, had written several articles defending the rights of Japanese American citizens. In one article, he wrote, "Is citizenship such a light and transient thing ... which is our ... right in normal times can be torn from us in times of war?" He was one of very few Japanese Americans who challenged relocation once it began.

The evacuees usually spent several months in the assembly centers, waiting to receive their permanent assignment to internment camps. The government created the War Relocation Authority (WRA), a civilian agency, to run the camps. The first head of the WRA was Milton Eisenhower. He was the brother of General Dwight D. Eisenhower, who later commanded the Allied forces in Europe and in 1952 became president of the United States.

Milton Eisenhower picked out 10 sites for relocation camps. Eight were in isolated areas of the West—Tule Lake and Manzanar, California; Minidoka, Idaho; Poston and Gila River, Arizona; Heart Mountain, Wyoming; and Granada, Colorado. Two camps, Jerome and Rohwer, were in Arkansas. The camps were built far from roads and railways, so if any of the internees escaped, they would have trouble reaching a town. Outside the camps, soldiers patrolled the grounds, while inside, private security guards carrying guns watched over the internees.

Upon arriving at the camps, the internees saw simple wooden barracks surrounded by barbed wire. At the mountain camps in Idaho, Wyoming, and Colorado, winter temperatures could reach minus 30 degrees Fahrenheit (minus 34 Celsius). At the desert camps in Arizona, temperatures often soared above 100 degrees F (38 degrees C), and sandstorms kept the internees inside their barracks. Whole families lived in spaces 20 feet (6 meters) wide and from 8 to 24 feet (2.4 to 7.3 m) long.

41

Japanese American Internment Camps

Legend:
◆ Internment camp
▇ Military exclusion area

CANADA

Wash.
Oregon
Tule Lake
Minidoka
Idaho
Heart Mountain
Montana
Wyoming
North Dakota
South Dakota
Minn.
Wisconsin
Mich.
Nevada
Topaz
Utah
Manzanar
California
Colorado
Granada
Nebraska
Iowa
Illinois
Ind.
Ohio
Missouri
Kansas
Kentucky
Tennessee
Arizona
Poston
Gila River
New Mexico
Oklahoma
Arkansas
Rohwer
Jerome
Miss.
Ala.
Ga.
Texas
La.
Fla.

PACIFIC OCEAN

MEXICO

Gulf of Mexico

0   200   400 mi.
0   200   400 km

Japanese American internment camps were mostly located in the West.

The walls of these "apartments" did not reach the ceilings, so sounds and smells easily drifted from one space to another. None of the apartments had running water. Throughout the camps, people got sick from eating food that had spoiled in the heat.

The internees tried to deal as best they could with harsh living conditions and their loss of freedom. They did their best to copy the lives they had lived on the outside. The adults held jobs in the camps, though even the most highly skilled, such as doctors, earned only about $19 per month—

much less than what they had earned before the war. The camps had their own farms and hospitals, and workers also cleaned, cooked, and sewed for other internees.

More than half of the detainees at the internment camps were children. They attended schools inside the camps where internees as well as non-Japanese American teachers taught, and the high schools held dances and other events that typical high schools would have. Together, families attended religious services and celebrated holidays and other special events. The camps had their own libraries and newspapers, though government officials reviewed the articles before they were

LIVING AT TULE LAKE

One of the young Nisei internees at the Tule Lake, California, internment camp was George Takei. He later became an actor and played Mr. Sulu in the original *Star Trek* television series and films. He described some of his experiences at Tule Lake:

Here there was gritty gravel and cutting little shards of hard fossils and rocks. ... We had come to a harsh landscape barren of any foliage except for the spiny tumbleweeds that rolled aimlessly around the stark, flat surface. ... Life in the camp was usually boring ... [b]ut the mess hall was the social focal point and cultural center of the block. ... Sometimes, after dinner, movies were shown in the mess hall. A big white sheet would be hung up at one end and a bulky, black projection machine set up at the opposite end. Because we were right across [from the mess hall], we always had the best seats.

43

Dinner was served in a large mess hall at Heart Mountain Relocation Center in Wyoming.

printed. Boys and young men played baseball or football, some young women played softball, and older men played board games.

Some internees were fortunate in that their stay in the camps was short. Even as new people arrived, some were allowed to leave. With so many men going off to fight in the war, farmers needed help picking their crops. Starting in May 1942, a few internees were allowed to go from an Oregon assembly center to a nearby farm. They lived in a government-run camp that did not have barbed wire or guards. As the year went on, about 10,000 people were allowed to leave the internment camps to help farmers.

Total Population of Internment Camps	
January 1, 1943	107,000
January 1, 1944	93,000
January 1, 1945	80,000
August 1945	58,000
December 1, 1945	12,545 (all at Tule Lake)
March 1, 1946	2,806 (all at Tule Lake)

Most had to return to the camps after the harvest, but a few were allowed to remain free on the farms. During 1942, some Nisei college students also received permission to leave the camps so they could finish their studies at such schools as the University of Idaho and the University of Nebraska.

Some historians believe the camp experience may have benefited some Japanese Americans. In their hometowns, prejudice might have kept them from holding certain jobs, and students might have been kept off of sports teams. In the camps, adults could hold important jobs and serve as leaders, and students could play sports or pursue other interests. But nothing could change the fact that they had lost their freedom and that their internment took away the legal rights they held under the U.S. Constitution. Most of those who were interned had no idea when they would be released from the camps, or what they would find when they returned home.

Proving Their Loyalty

Chapter

5

Just as the wartime need for farm workers helped some Japanese Americans gain permission to leave the camps, the fighting itself offered freedom for several thousand young, male Nisei. Before the attack on Pearl Harbor, about 3,000 Nisei had been drafted into the U.S. military. Others had volunteered to serve. But when the United States entered World War II, some of these soldiers were discharged because of fears they would be disloyal to the United States. The U.S. government also refused to let any more Japanese Americans volunteer to defend the country, even though there was no evidence that any Japanese Americans already serving had been disloyal.

By the middle of 1942, however, the U.S. military realized it needed thousands of people who could speak fluent Japanese. They would be able to translate enemy documents and radio messages and question prisoners of war. The War Department began recruiting volunteers from the internment camps. They first looked for Japanese Americans called Kibei—Nisei who had spent time studying in Japan. Then they broadened their search, desperate for any Nisei who could speak even the most basic Japanese. Eventually, about 6,000 internees were sent to learn Japanese at the Military Intelligence Service Language School at Camp Savage or Fort Snelling, both in Minnesota. Most of these specially trained soldiers served in Asia. They were called noncombatants, meaning that they served behind the lines and did not fight. Some, however, did see military action, and nine Japanese Americans died during battles.

U.S. Army interpreters translated papers found on wounded Japanese soldiers.

The Nisei who joined the Military Intelligence Service filled a special need. But as the year 1942 went on, U.S. officials such as Milton Eisenhower and Assistant Secretary of War John McCloy thought that Japanese Americans should be allowed to volunteer for combat units. In its propaganda, Japan claimed that the Americans were racists because of their internment of Japanese Americans. U.S. officials wanted to show that the U.S. government was not racist. Eisenhower wrote to President Roosevelt: "We can combat [Japan's propaganda] with counter propaganda only if our deeds permit us to tell the truth." The way to do that, he argued, was to let the Nisei join the military. Some U.S. officials also wanted to boost the morale of the large majority of internees who remained loyal to the United States. Letting Nisei fight, they hoped, would lift the spirits of their friends and relatives still in the camps.

Some military leaders opposed the plan, but in January 1943, the president agreed with several of his advisers that volunteers considered loyal would be allowed to join the U.S. Army. Government

BEHIND ENEMY LINES

Roy Matsumoto was a Kibei sent to the internment camp in Jerome, Arkansas. While there, he volunteered for military service. After receiving his basic military training, he entered the Military Intelligence Service. He then volunteered to join "Merrill's Marauders," an Army unit that was specially trained to work in enemy territory. On one mission, Matsumoto sneaked behind enemy lines and heard Japanese forces planning an attack on the Marauders. This information helped the Americans prepare for an ambush on the Japanese.

officials devised a written test that could be used to assess the volunteers' loyalty. The test asked a series of questions about their loyalty to the United States and their feelings about Japan. Members of the FBI and Army officials also questioned the volunteers before they were cleared to serve.

Internees who wanted to serve in the military had to go through a process called swearing in. Like all soldiers, they promised to obey orders and defend the country.

49

More than 1,000 Nisei passed the loyalty test, left the internment camps, and joined the 442nd Regimental Combat Team. Nisei from Hawaii also volunteered, and many of them served in the 100th Infantry Battalion, which merged into the 442nd Regiment in 1944. The regiment's motto was "Go for broke," suggesting the troops would do whatever they had to do to defeat the enemy. The first Japanese American soldiers saw combat action in September 1943. For the remainder of the war, the 442nd Regiment fought in Italy, France, and Germany, with almost one-third of the men killed or wounded.

The heroics of the 442nd Regiment proved that many Japanese Americans were loyal citizens. The decision to let the volunteers fight, however, led to problems for some internees who remained in the camps. The government began to administer

BRAVERY UNDER FIRE

The 442nd Regimental Combat Unit ended World War II as the most decorated U.S. Army unit ever. Its members won more than 9,000 Purple Hearts, medals given to soldiers wounded during battle. The soldiers of the 442nd also won nearly 5,000 medals given for bravery during combat and other important military service. During the war, one Nisei, Sadao Munemori, received the country's highest military decoration, the Medal of Honor. More than 50 years after the war ended, President Bill Clinton recognized the service of 20 more Japanese American veterans of World War II by giving them Medals of Honor as well.

the loyalty test to all internees over the age of 17 to see whether they could be trusted to leave the camps to work. The loyalty test would also be used to resettle some internees. President Roosevelt and his advisers decided that some Japanese Americans would be freed from the camps but relocated to cities far from the West Coast.

Japanese American soldiers fought on the front lines in Europe during World War II.

Two questions on the test troubled some internees. Question 27 asked, "Are you willing to serve in the Armed Forces of the United States on combat duty, wherever ordered?" Question 28 asked whether the Japanese Americans would "swear ... allegiance to the United States" and end all "allegiance or obedience to the Japanese emperor, or any other foreign government."

Both questions upset the Issei and Nisei, for different reasons. With the first question, some members of both groups felt they were being asked to risk their lives without being given any guarantee that their legal rights would be restored once they left the camp. Question 28 seemed to be asking the Issei to denounce their Japanese citizenship. Since the United States would not grant them citizenship, doing so would mean that they were not citizens of any country. Question 28 also seemed to suggest they had allegiance to Japan's emperor, when they already considered themselves loyal Americans. They felt the government was considering them guilty until proven innocent—the opposite of the way the U.S. justice system is supposed to work. The assumption that they might be disloyal angered some Nisei. Under those conditions, one Nisei later wrote, "It is not surprising some Nisei felt compelled to refuse to declare their loyalty."

In some camps, the internees' leaders met to discuss how the questions should be answered. Kibei and Issei who supported Japan encouraged the Nisei to answer "no" to Questions 27 and 28. Some Kibei saw such an answer as a protest of the treatment Japanese Americans had received since Pearl Harbor.

The Japanese American Citizens League told the internees they should answer "yes," and in the end, most of the internees did. The ones who answered "no," for whatever reason, were labeled disloyal to the United States. Nicknamed "no-nos" and "no-no boys," they were sent to the camp at Tule Lake, which already had a number of internees who were considered disloyal. At the same time, most of the "loyal" residents of Tule Lake were moved to other camps. About 4,000 remained, however, because they did not want to be relocated again.

QUESTIONING LOYALTIES

In December 1942, well before the loyalty test was given to internees, internal divisions led to violence at the internment camp in Manzanar, California. Some Issei and Kibei in the camp disliked Nisei who belonged to the JACL. Members were given the best jobs, and some Kibei and Issei resented the members' close relationship with camp officials. In December 1942, one Kibei, Harry Ueno, was accused of beating up a JACL leader and was arrested and removed from the camp. He was later returned to the camp but kept under arrest in the camp jail. Angry that Ueno was still under arrest, several thousand internees protested this action, leading to violence. Some of the protesters taunted military police at the camp; some also threw rocks. The police responded by firing at the protesters, killing two internees.

By the summer of 1943, Tule Lake became the sole camp for so-called disloyal Japanese Americans and their families. It soon became the largest camp, holding more than 18,000 people. To preserve order, the government built new fences and watchtowers and sent eight tanks. Still, trouble sometimes broke out at Tule Lake.

In October, a group of farm workers at Tule Lake went on strike, demanding better working

At Manzanar, some internees showed their loyalty by taking part in Memorial Day ceremonies, which honored veterans of previous wars.

conditions. The strikers became angry when replacement Japanese American workers were brought in from other camps and given higher pay. On November 1, the Army used tear gas to break up a large crowd that had gathered to protest the sending of camp supplies to the replacement workers.

For a time, Tule Lake was placed under martial law. To some Americans who still distrusted the internees, the Tule Lake "riot" was proof they still could not be trusted. Even one government aide at first believed a false report that 500 armed internees had taken a civilian official as a prisoner. Still, as 1944 went on, many Japanese Americans proved their loyalty by fighting bravely in the military and living peacefully outside the camps—even while friends and relatives remained behind barbed wire. ◣

The Battle Against Internment

Although the Japanese Americans proved their loyalty during World War II, most of them felt they should not have been forced to do so. Before the attack on Pearl Harbor, Japanese Americans were known as people who lived peacefully, worked hard, and obeyed the law. The attack on Pearl Harbor, however, led to questions about loyalty—and internment.

From the start, not all Americans welcomed the camps. Some presidential advisers believed they were not necessary, given the reports suggesting that most Issei and Nisei were loyal. Most of the arguments against the camps happened behind closed doors, and few people publicly spoke out against internment. In some cases, however, the fight against internment was very public, and it led all the way to the U.S. Supreme Court.

The legal challenges to internment reached the U.S. Supreme Court in Washington, D.C.

One group that did speak out was the American Civil Liberties Union (ACLU), an organization that defends people or groups whose constitutional rights have been denied. In 1942, soon after Roosevelt issued Executive Order 9066, the ACLU released a statement that said giving the military the power to exclude citizens and aliens from certain zones could lead to "the most serious violation of civil rights since the war began." The ACLU argued that the only fair actions would be to place all citizens in the zones under martial law or hold hearings for individual Japanese Americans so they could prove their loyalty. The government, however, ignored these suggestions.

Despite its opposition to Executive Order 9066, the ACLU was not prepared to challenge Roosevelt's power to issue it. The group decided instead to

LETTERS TO THE WHITE HOUSE

Some Americans protested Executive Order 9066 by writing to President Roosevelt at the White House. One letter came from a group called the Post War World Council. Its members opposed war and racism. One of the most famous signers of the letter was John Dewey, a scholar who called for improving U.S. education and promoting democracy. He and the others who sent the letter called on Roosevelt to end the relocation, which they compared to "the ... theory of justice practiced by the Nazis [German government] in their treatment of the Jews." The members did not realize at the time, however, what the Germans were doing to the Jews and others held in their concentration camps. The German camps were death camps where millions of people were killed—a much more horrific internment experience than what Japanese Americans faced in the U.S. camps.

challenge specific aspects of the military's tactics in carrying out the order. On the West Coast, the ACLU soon became involved in two important legal cases related to the relocation.

Under General DeWitt's orders, a curfew took effect on March 27, 1942, in Military Area #1—the western regions of California, Arizona, Washington, and Oregon. The curfew began before most Japanese Americans left for the assembly centers, and it applied only to enemy aliens and the Nisei. At the time, Gordon Hirabayashi, a Nisei, was a student at the University of Washington. He was also a Quaker, a Protestant religion that opposes all war and prejudice against any group. Hirabayashi was arrested for ignoring both the curfew and the order to go to an assembly center. Hirabayashi actively

Gordon Hirabayashi was a student who lived in Seattle, Washington, in 1942.

59

sought arrest because he wanted to test the legality of the evacuation order and the curfew. He said, "I must maintain the democratic standards for which this nation lives."

In October, Hirabayashi was found guilty on both counts and sentenced to three months in jail. His case, however, was not over. Hirabayashi appealed the decision in his trial to a federal court called the Court of Appeals. That court asked the U.S. Supreme Court for advice on points of law in the case, and the Supreme Court then decided to handle the appeal itself.

The Supreme Court decided Hirabayashi's case in June 1943. All nine justices agreed that Hirabayashi was fairly tried and found guilty. The government had the power to impose a curfew that was limited to enemy aliens and the Nisei. The court did not directly address whether the president had the power to issue Executive Order 9066 in the first place.

Justice Harlan Stone wrote the opinion in *Hirabayashi v. United States*. He outlined some reasons why the U.S. government could create a curfew that targeted mostly Japanese Americans. They had, he wrote, "a continued attachment ... to Japan and Japanese institutions," rather than to the United States. The government had no way of knowing, he continued, whether Nisei were loyal to the United States, and so it could take broad measures against all of them.

One justice originally did not accept the trial court's decisions. Justice Frank Murphy wanted to vote against the Supreme Court's decision. But Justice Felix Frankfurter convinced him that the court should reach a unanimous decision in such an important case. Otherwise, Frankfurter said, the court would be "playing into the hands of the enemy." Murphy went along with the decision, but he wrote a separate statement, saying, "The broad guarantees of ... the Constitution protecting essential liberties are [not] suspended by the mere existence of a state of war."

Frank Murphy served on the U.S. Supreme Court from 1940 to 1949.

More than a year later, in December 1944, the Supreme Court decided another case involving the evacuation order. In 1942, Fred Korematsu had defied the order to evacuate Military Area #1. He changed his name and tried to pass himself off as a Mexican American. Eventually, however, he was arrested, found guilty, and sent to an internment camp. The Supreme Court again ruled that the U.S. government had the legal right to order Nisei out of certain areas during wartime. The court said that singling out Japanese Americans for evacuation and internment was not racist. But once again, it did not directly rule on whether the government had the legal right to send Japanese Americans to internment camps.

This time, however, the decision was not unanimous. Three justices supported Korematsu. Murphy said the internment was based on misinformation and half-truths spread by Americans prejudiced against Japanese Americans. Justice Robert Jackson said he would have released Korematsu immediately if he could. In legal discussions of Japanese American internment, this case and *Hirabayashi v. United States* are usually noted together. They show that the court had several chances to strike down Executive Order 9066, yet chose not to. Still, over time, some members of the court began to change their views on internment, as another important case showed.

On the same day the Supreme Court decided

Korematsu v. United States, it also settled the case of Mitsuye Endo. A Nisei, Endo had obeyed orders to go to the Tanforan assembly center and the camps at Tule Lake, California, and Topaz, Utah. But soon after her internment, she filed a legal request called *habeas corpus*. This Latin phrase means "show the body," and if the request is granted, the government must let people being held against their will take their case to court and plead for their freedom. Endo claimed that she was a loyal U.S. citizen who had not broken any laws and was being held in the camps against her will. The government admitted that she was loyal and lawful but claimed it had the right to hold her because of Executive Order 9066 and the law Congress had passed to enforce it.

OTHER KINDS OF RESISTANCE

In January 1944, the U.S. government began drafting for military service any Nisei who had passed the loyalty test, even if they were still in the camps. Across the camps, some young men protested their continued internment—and that of their families—by refusing to enter the military. The protest that began at the camp in Heart Mountain, Wyoming, produced 85 resisters—the largest group of them. They and other protesters went to jail for their acts. Most men at Heart Mountain and the other camps, however, obeyed their draft orders. Both the ACLU and JACL thought Nisei internees had a legal duty to obey the draft. In 2000, however, the JACL changed its position and offered an apology to the resisters for not supporting their efforts to protest internment.

Mitsuye Endo felt that she, like many other loyal Japanese Americans, was being held illegally in the camps.

In another unanimous decision, the Supreme Court ruled that Endo was being held by the War Relocation Authority, not the military. As a civilian organization, the WRA did not have the legal power to hold Endo once she was evacuated from the military areas and had proven that she was not a threat to the country's security. The court ordered her release from Topaz.

In Mitsuye Endo's case, called *Ex Parte Mitsuye Endo* ("On Behalf of Mitsuye Endo"), Justice William O. Douglas wrote the majority decision for the Supreme Court. His decision said, in part:

> *A citizen who is concededly loyal presents no problem of espionage or sabotage. Loyalty is a matter of the heart and mind not of race, creed, or color. He who is loyal is by definition not a spy or a saboteur. When the power to detain is derived from the power to protect the war effort against espionage and sabotage, detention which has no relationship to that objective is unauthorized.*

The decision in Endo's case would now apply to thousands of other people like her: Nisei who were loyal and posed no threat to the United States. The time of the internment camps was coming to an end.

Closing Down the Camps

Even before the *Endo* decision, some members of the U.S. government wanted to end the policies affecting Japanese Americans. By spring 1944, the Allies were almost ready to launch a major attack in Europe against Germany. In the Pacific, the Allies had driven the Japanese from several islands they had captured. U.S. planes would later use those islands as bases for bombing raids on Japan. U.S. leaders increasingly felt that the Allies would win the war, and the concerns about Japanese Americans were fading.

Furthermore, the Nisei who had already left the camps to fight for the 442nd Regiment, attend college, or work on farms and in factories had proven their loyalty. By now, the camps held about 80,000 internees, down from a peak of 107,000 in 1943.

At this time, Harold Ickes was one of President Roosevelt's top advisers. He ran the Department of the Interior, which had taken control of the War Relocation Authority early in 1944. Ickes had said almost two years before that he did not "like the idea of loyal citizens … being kept in relocation centers any longer than need be." Now he and his aides began to call for ending the ban on Japanese Americans in the military areas of the West Coast.

As the Allies gained control in World War II, fewer Japanese Americans remained in internment camps, such as Manzanar, in California.

67

They also began the process of closing the camps. With fewer internees, the government needed fewer camps, and the camp in Jerome, Arkansas, was shut down in June 1944. Other members of the government, however, resisted efforts to release internees, and reports of the Tule Lake riot kept alive the prejudice some Americans had against the Japanese living in the United States.

President Roosevelt was also sensitive to public feelings about the internees. He was hoping to win his fourth presidential election in the fall. He did not want to alienate voters on the West Coast who still hated and feared Japanese Americans. Some internees had already been resettled far from the West Coast, and Roosevelt wanted to continue that practice as internees were released. If they were spread out, Roosevelt believed, they would seem less threatening to other Americans. And resettled Japanese Americans would go to areas that did not have a history of anti-Japanese feelings, as the West Coast did.

The Supreme Court decision in *Ex Parte Endo* led to slow changes for the internees. The ruling meant that all Nisei who had passed the loyalty test were free to leave the camps and return to their homes on the West Coast. The government had already decided in December 1944 to end the exclusion order and let the Nisei return to the West Coast. Some, however, were afraid of how they would be treated when they returned. One Nisei from Seattle, Washington, reported to friends still in the camp that he faced prejudice when he went home. Nevertheless, by the spring of 1945, the pace of resettlement in California and the rest of the West Coast had increased. The Nisei were happy with their release, but many had to leave behind Issei friends and relatives who had to remain in the camps.

On April 12, 1945, President Roosevelt died, and Vice President Harry Truman became president. A few weeks later, on May 7, 1945, the fighting ended

Harry S. Truman became the 33rd president of the United States in 1945.

69

in Europe. Truman then focused on ending the war with Japan, and he made the decision to use the most powerful weapon known at that time: the atomic bomb. Although he was deeply troubled

In August 1945, the United States dropped atomic bombs on the Japanese cities of Hiroshima and Nagasaki.

with the idea of killing tens of thousands of Japanese civilians, Truman believed that bombing Japan would force the country to surrender, saving the Allies from launching a ground invasion against their Asian enemy.

On August 6 and 9, 1945, the United States dropped atomic bombs on the Japanese cities of Hiroshima and Nagasaki. On September 2, less than a month later, the Japanese surrendered. As World War II came to an end, most of the remaining 44,000 internees knew they would soon be going home. U.S. officials had already told camp leaders that the camps would be shut within one year of the war's end. In reality, all the camps except Tule Lake were closed by the end of 1945.

Japanese Americans wanted the War Relocation Authority to help them as they returned to life outside the camps. Japanese Americans asked for loans or other aid so they could replace the items they had sold before leaving for the camps. The government refused. Instead it gave each family $50 and a train ride back to where they had been picked up before entering the camps. With their farms and businesses gone, some people had nothing to return

RESETTLEMENT CITIES

Starting in 1943, several major U.S. cities welcomed internees who were allowed to leave the camps but were still banned from living on the West Coast. Some stayed in the region and moved to Colorado, Utah, and Idaho. By November 1944, the largest number—approximately 8,000—had settled in Illinois, with most going to Chicago. Cincinnati, Ohio, was another Midwest city that attracted a large number of released internees. Both cities offered jobs and less prejudice than Japanese Americans met with in the West.

to, so they tried to stay in the camps as long as they could. The government eventually packed up their belongings for them and forced them to leave.

Tule Lake, which held the so-called disloyal Japanese Americans, was the last to close. All remaining internees left in March 1946. About 5,000 of the internees there had decided to go to Japan instead of returning to their homes on

After the war, a Japanese American couple who had been held at Gila River in Arizona went back to California and opened a restaurant.

the West Coast. Many of these people were Nisei who felt betrayed by the United States because of the wartime relocation. They chose to give up their U.S. citizenship.

The Japanese Americans who went back to the West Coast found life almost as hard outside the camps as it had been inside. Many had lost their farms, and the government had sold their tractors

73

President Truman (left) inspected the 442nd Regimental Combat Team and honored the troops after they distinguished themselves in Europe during World War II.

74

and other equipment to Caucasian farmers. Some returned to face neighbors who angrily suggested they should go to Japan, and violence against returning Japanese Americans was not uncommon. A California newspaper, the *Watsonville Register-Pajaronian*, reported that "unidentified persons threw or shot a flare toward the Buddhist temple ...

which is being used as a hostel by the Japanese."

The treatment the returning internees received upset President Truman, who believed the camps themselves should never have been used. Years after leaving the White House, he told a writer:

> *They were concentration camps. They called it relocation, but they put them in concentration camps, and I was against it. We were in a period of emergency, but it was still the wrong thing to do. It was one place where I never went along with Roosevelt. He never should have allowed it. … People out on the West Coast got scared, and they panicked. … What a leader has to do is stop the panic.*

In 1946, Truman tried to show his admiration for the Japanese Americans after their wartime experience. He invited members of the 442nd Regiment to the White House. Truman said to the soldiers, "You fought not only the enemy, but you fought prejudice—and you have won." But the Issei and Nisei still had other battles ahead of them as they tried to regain some of what they had lost because of internment. ◣

Righting a Wrong

Chapter

8

President Truman thought the country should do something for the Japanese Americans who had been sent to the camps. In 1948, he called on Congress to pass the Japanese American Claims Act. The law was designed to repay the internees for some of the property they lost before their evacuation. At times the government fought claims for payment, and in the end, the internees received only about 10 percent of the value of the property they had lost.

One positive change for Japanese Americans came in 1952. That year, Congress passed the McCarran-Walter Act, a law that ended restrictions on Japanese immigration in place since 1924. The law also said that the Issei and new Japanese immigrants could become naturalized U.S. citizens.

Kaun Onodera left the Minidoka internment camp to join the 442nd Regiment. Years later, he proudly displayed the Bronze Star he earned for his bravery.

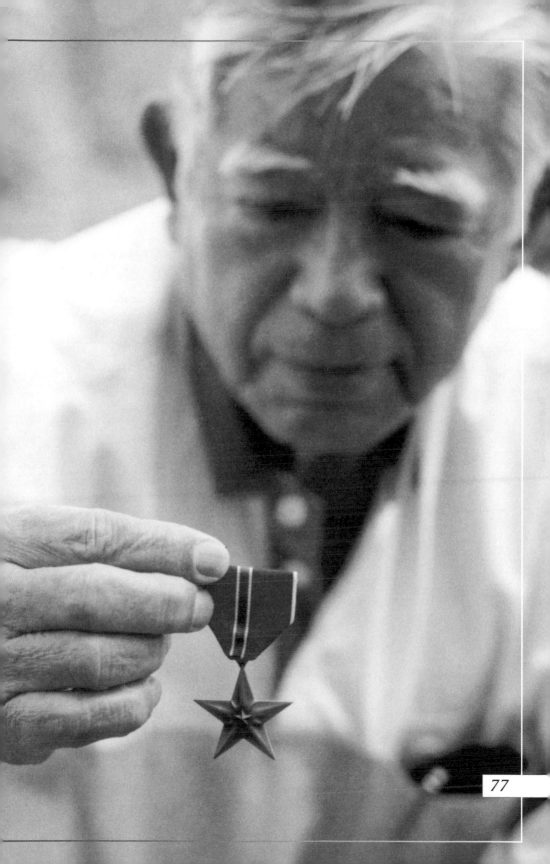

For the next few decades, many former internees quietly rebuilt their lives. Once again they tried to show that they were loyal Americans. As the son of one internee put it, "They didn't talk about internment—they really buried it deep within their soul."

But some of the Nisei still felt bitterness over how they had been treated. In 1970, members of the JACL asked the U.S. government to pay reparations. This money would go to anyone who had been in the camps. A decade later, Congress agreed to study the treatment of Japanese Americans during World War II, which was a first step toward considering reparations.

It wasn't until 1976 that Executive Order 9066 was repealed. That year was the 200th anniversary of the founding of the United States. President Gerald Ford noted that while the country had much to celebrate, it should also remember its national mistakes. In his official statement, Ford said:

A Long Order

Executive Order 9066's power to evict people from their homes ended with World War II. In a legal sense, however, the order remained in effect for many years because no president had formally ended it.

> *We now know what we should have known then—not only was that evacuation wrong, but Japanese Americans were and are loyal Americans. ... We have learned from the tragedy of that long-ago experience forever to treasure liberty and justice for each individual American.*

In 1980, the Commission on Wartime Relocation and Internment of Civilians (CWRIC) was formed to investigate the treatment of Japanese Americans during World War II. It held hearings in cities across the United States, seeking information from former internees. Almost two years later, the commission issued its report to Congress. It found that President Roosevelt's decision to intern the Japanese Americans "followed a long and ugly history of West Coast anti-Japanese agitation and legislation." The report also included some Nisei's memories of life in the camps. One said:

> *I learned to salute the flag by the time I was five years old. I was learning, as best one could learn in Manzanar, what it meant to live in America. But, I was also learning the sometimes bitter price one has to pay for it.*

In 1983, CWRIC recommended that the U.S. government pay $20,000 to each living internee. That same year, Fred Korematsu and Gordon Hirabayashi challenged the decisions made in their wartime legal battles. They were joined by Minori Yasui, who during the war had also brought a case challenging internment to the Supreme Court. He died before the final decision could be reached in this new round of legal proceedings.

Korematsu and Hirabayashi had learned that government officials had lied or withheld evidence during their earlier legal cases. The Supreme Court had ruled against Korematsu and the others based

Fred Korematsu (left), Minori Yasui (center), and Gordon Hirabayashi filed petitions in U.S. district courts in 1983 asking that their cases be reopened.

on this false and missing evidence. The men outlined their evidence in a statement to a federal court, hoping to have the earlier decisions reversed. In Korematsu's statement, his lawyers concluded by saying:

> *It would be impossible to find any other instance in American history of such a long standing, pervasive and unlawful governmental scheme designed to mislead and defraud the courts and the nation.*

Korematsu believed that other innocent Americans could be held in prison or concentration camps without a trial or a hearing if his wartime conviction was allowed to stand.

For Korematsu, the federal court's decision came in 1984, while Hirabayashi had to wait until 1987 to get a final decision. In the end, both men won their arguments, and their original convictions were overturned. In the eyes of the court, they were innocent. The judge in Korematsu's case ended her opinion with these thoughts:

> *[The Korematsu case] stands as a caution that in times of [war], our institutions ... must be prepared to protect all citizens from the petty fears and prejudices that are so easily aroused.*

Korematsu came to be seen as a hero in the struggle to protect the liberties all citizens enjoy under the U.S. Constitution. In 1998, President Bill Clinton gave him the Presidential Medal of Freedom, the highest honor the U.S. government gives to civilians. Korematsu died in 2005.

After Hirabayashi's conviction was overturned in 1987, Congress finally took action on the CWRIC report. In 1988, the lawmakers agreed to give each internee $20,000. By that time, about 60,000 were still alive. The first payment, made in 1990 under President George H.W. Bush, went to the oldest surviving internee, 107-year-old Mamoru Eto.

Along with the check came an apology. Former internee Suyako Kitashima attended the ceremony. "I just broke down," she later said. "[For] many old people, the mere fact that the president apologized is what they were living for."

In a written public apology, President Bush said:

> *We can never fully right the wrongs of the past. But we can take a clear stand for justice and recognize that serious injustices were done to Japanese Americans during World War II.*

The reparation payments given to former internees, which totaled $1.6 billion, continued until 1999. By then, internment was a distant memory to many Americans.

The internment of Japanese Americans during

THE CAMPS TODAY

After the war, most of the buildings at the internment camps were taken down or moved to other sites. The land was either sold back to the previous owners or turned over to various U.S. government agencies. Over the years, buildings left behind at the camps began to fall apart, and many people might have forgotten about the camps and their wartime role. Today, however, signs and monuments inform visitors to the campsites about Japanese American internment. The U.S. government lists six of the 10 camps as historically important places, and Manzanar is a National Historic Site. The camp has exhibits and shows a film explaining the relocation process during World War II.

World War II addressed a genuine fear. After the bombing of Pearl Harbor, Japan seemed a real threat to the mainland of the United States. Many Americans thought Japanese Americans would be more loyal to their former homeland than to the United States. Though government reports stressed that most Japanese Americans were loyal, President

Today, the Manzanar Relocation Center that held nearly 10,000 Japanese Americans during World War II is marked by a simple monument.

Roosevelt listened to advisers who were swept up in the fear. The internment forced families from their homes and denied U.S. citizens their freedom.

Though decades later the U.S. government and the courts admitted that internment had been a mistake, the admission came too late to satisfy the men, women, and children who were forced

A group of Japanese Americans who were unable to complete high school because of their internment were awarded honorary diplomas 60 years later.

to live behind barbed wire. The Japanese American experience during World War II still has a powerful impact on the lives of the surviving internees and their families. And it reminds all Americans that protecting civil liberties is a constant struggle, especially during a time of war. ◣

Timeline

June 8, 1869

A group of Japanese immigrants settles in California.

October 11, 1906

Officials in San Francisco put Japanese American and Caucasian children in separate schools.

February 1907

President Theodore Roosevelt begins working on the Gentlemen's Agreement, which limits the number of Japanese immigrants allowed to enter the country.

May 3, 1913

The Alien Land Law passes both houses of the California Legislature.

November 3, 1920

A new California law makes it harder for Issei to own land in their children's names.

November 3, 1922

In *Ozawa v. United States*, the U.S. Supreme Court rules that Issei cannot become naturalized citizens.

May 6, 1924

President Calvin Coolidge signs into law a bill that ends almost all immigration from Japan.

September 18, 1931

Japan invades Manchuria, a region of China.

October 2, 1941

President Franklin Roosevelt receives a report stating that most Japanese Americans would remain loyal to the United States if the country went to war with Japan.

December 7, 1941

Japan launches a surprise attack on the U.S. Navy base at Pearl Harbor, Hawaii; the U.S. government begins arresting Japanese Americans considered dangerous enemy aliens.

February 19, 1942

President Roosevelt issues Executive Order 9066, which gives the military the power to remove anyone from parts of the country called military areas.

March 2, 1942

General John DeWitt declares California and parts of three other states as Military Area #1; the first evacuations to assembly centers begin by the end of the month.

March 18, 1942

The War Relocation Authority is created.

March 27, 1942

A curfew takes effect in Military Area #1.

May 1942

U.S. officials let some internees leave assembly centers to help farmers raise their crops.

May 30, 1942

Fred Korematsu ignores evacuation orders and is later arrested.

October 20, 1942

Gordon Hirabayashi is found guilty of breaking the curfew and refusing to report for relocation.

December 6, 1942

Violence erupts at the Manzanar, California, camp, leading to the death of two internees.

January 1, 1943

The U.S. Army reverses an earlier decision that rejected recruiting Nisei into the military.

June 21, 1943

In *Hirabayashi v. United States*, the U.S. Supreme Court rules that the curfew in Military Area #1 and the relocation of Japanese Americans are legal.

September 29, 1943

Japanese American soldiers see their first action in Italy.

November 1, 1943

The U.S. government uses tear gas to end an internee protest at Tule Lake, California.

June 30, 1944

Jerome, Arkansas, is the first internment camp to close.

December 18, 1944

In *Korematsu v. United States*, the U.S. Supreme Court again rules that the evacuation order was legal, but several justices question the decision; the court also rules in *Ex Parte Endo* that the government cannot keep loyal Japanese American citizens from returning to their homes on the West Coast.

May 7, 1945

World War II ends in Europe.

August 15, 1945

Japan announces its surrender, ending World War II.

October 1945

Camps close in Granada, Colorado, Minidoka, Idaho, and Topaz, California.

November 1945

Camps close in Gila River, Arizona, Heart Mountain, Wyoming, Manzanar, California, Poston, Arizona, and Rowher, Arkansas.

March 20, 1946

Tule Lake, California, is the last internment camp to close.

Timeline

June 30, 1946

The War Relocation Authority is dissolved.

July 2, 1948

Congress passes the Japanese American Claims Act, repaying internees for some of the property they lost before and during their internment.

June 30, 1952

Congress passes a law that lets Japanese immigrants enter the country and become naturalized citizens.

July 10, 1970

A California chapter of the Japanese American Citizens League asks Congress to consider paying reparations to former internees.

February 19, 1976

President Gerald Ford repeals Executive Order 9066.

July 14, 1981

The Commission on Wartime Relocation and Internment of Civilians (CWRIC) holds hearings on the experience of internees.

June 16, 1983

CWRIC recommends that Congress give each living internee $20,000.

July 14, 1984

A federal court overturns Fred Korematsu's earlier conviction for ignoring the evacuation order.

September 24, 1987

A federal court overturns Gordon Hirabayashi's conviction for ignoring the evacuation order.

1989

The U.S. government makes its first reparation payments to internees.

January 15, 1998

President Bill Clinton gives Fred Korematsu the Presidential Medal of Freedom for his efforts to fight wartime internment.

January 15, 1999

The U.S. government ends its reparations program for Japanese American internees.

On the Web

For more information on this topic, use FactHound.

1 Go to *www.facthound.com*

2 Type in this book ID: 0756524539

3 Click on the *Fetch It* button. FactHound will find the best Web sites for you.

Historic Sites

Japanese American National Museum
369 East First St.
Los Angeles, CA 90012
213/625-0414

This museum tells the history of Japanese Americans through its exhibits and events.

Minidoka Internment National Monument
221 MN State St.
Hagerman, ID 83332
208/837-4793

This former location of an internment camp was recently named a national monument.

Look For More Books in This Series

Brown v. Board of Education:
The Case for Integration

The Chinese Revolution:
The Triumph of Communism

The Democratic Party:
America's Oldest Party

The Indian Removal Act:
Forced Relocation

The Progressive Party:
The Success of a Failed Party

The Republican Party:
The Story of the Grand Old Party

The Scopes Trial:
The Battle Over Teaching Evolution

A complete list of **Snapshots in History** titles is available on our Web site: *www.compasspointbooks.com*

Glossary

aliens
citizens of one country who reside in another country

allies
friends or helpers; when capitalized, refers to the United States and its allies during major wars

civilians
people not part of a military force

civil rights
a person's rights that are guaranteed by the U.S. Constitution

Constitution
the document that describes the basic laws and principles by which the United States is governed

creed
a statement of basic beliefs

diplomats
people who represent communities or governments in their foreign affairs

discriminate
to treat a person or group unfairly, usually because of race

drafted
compelled by law to serve in the military

espionage
spying

evacuation
leaving a dangerous place to go somewhere safer

internment
the placement of an enemy or suspicious person under guard

naturalized
made a citizen of a country or state although born in a different country

prejudice
hatred or unfair treatment of a group of people who belong to a certain race or religion

propaganda
information or ideas that are deliberately spread among the public to try to influence its thinking

racism
the belief that one race is better than another

reparations
payments made to make amends for wrongdoing

repealed
officially canceled an existing law

sabotage
to damage, destroy, or interfere with on purpose

slur
an insulting name or word

unanimous
agreed upon by all parties

Source Notes

Chapter 1

Page 9, line 1: Yoshiko Uchida. *Desert Exile: The Uprooting of a Japanese American Family.* Seattle: University of Washington Press, 1982, p. 67.

Page 12, line 6: Ibid., p. 71.

Page 15, line 17: Greg Robinson. *By Order of the President: FDR and the Internment of Japanese Americans.* Cambridge, Mass.: Harvard University Press, 2001, p. 92.

Chapter 2

Page 20, line 10: William Petersen. *Japanese Americans.* Washington, D.C.: University Press of America, 1971, p. 32.

Page 20, line 22: Roger Daniels. *Coming to America: A History of Immigration and Ethnicity in American Life.* 2nd ed. New York: Perennial, 2002, p. 255.

Page 21, line 29: Roger Daniels. *Prisoners Without Trial: Japanese Americans in World War II.* Rev. ed. New York: Hill and Wang, 2004, p. 14.

Page 24, line 3: Robert Dallek. *Franklin D. Roosevelt and American Foreign Policy, 1932–1945.* New York: Oxford University Press, 1979, p. 75.

Page 24, line 12: *By Order of the President*, p. 49.

Chapter 3

Page 28, line 8: Ibid., p. 66.

Page 29, line 8: David Colbert, ed. *Eyewitness to America.* New York: Pantheon, 1997. p. 400.

Page 30, line 22: *By Order of the President*, p. 75.

Page 32, line 4: Douglas Brinkley, ed. *World War II: The Axis Assault, 1939–1942.* New York: Times Books, 2003, p. 279.

Page 33, line 3: *Prisoners Without Trial*, p. 35.

Page 34, line 21: "Chronology of 1942 San Francisco War Events." Virtual Museum of the City of San Francisco. 10 March 2006. www.sfmuseum.org/war/42.html

Page 35, line 15: *Prisoners Without Trial*, p. 145.

Chapter 4

Page 36, line 10: Ibid., p. 49.

Page 39, line 6: "Jap League Aids Exodus. 28 Feb. 1942." *PBS: Conscience and the Constitution.* 9 March 2006. www.pbs.org/itvs/conscience/compliance/better_americans/04_ap_i.html

Page 39, line 17: "Conference Report on H.R. 442, Civil Liberties Act of 1988." *Japanese American Curriculum.* 6 March 2006. http://bss.sfsu.edu/internment/Congressional%20Records/19880804.html#masaoka

Page 40, line 13: Chris Riggs. "On Japanese American Relocation and Internment During World War II," 2005. Lewis-Clark State College. 14 April 2006. www.lcsc.edu/criggs/documents/Internment.pdf, p. 41.

Page 43 sidebar: Lawson Fusao Inada, ed. *Only What We Could Carry: The Japanese American Internment Experience.* Berkeley, Calif.: Heyday Books, 2000, pp. 121, 123.

Source Notes

Chapter 5

Page 48, line 11: *By Order of the President*, p. 163.

Page 52, line 2: Ibid., p. 181.

Page 52, lines 5 and 7: *Only What We Could Carry*, p. 306.

Page 52, line 26: Ibid., p. 307.

Chapter 6

Page 58, line 8: R. Jeffrey Blair. "In Opposition to the Japanese Internment: The ACLU During World War II," 1999. Aichi Gakuin University. 8 March 2006. www.aichi-gakuin.ac.jp/~jeffreyb/research/ACLU.one.TextB.html#oppol

Page 58, sidebar: *By Order of the President*, p. 160.

Page 60, line 2: "In Opposition to the Japanese Internment."

Page 60, line 25: Peter Irons, ed. *Justice Delayed: The Record of the Japanese American Internment Cases.* Middletown, Conn.: Wesleyan University Press, 1989, p. 61.

Page 61, line 7: Ibid., p. 49.

Page 61, line 9: Ibid., p. 68.

Page 65, line 1: U.S. Supreme Court. "Ex Parte Mitsuye Endo." 18 Dec. 1944. FindLaw. 11 March 2006. http://caselaw.lp.findlaw.com/cgi-bin/getcase.pl?court=us&vol=323&invol=283

Chapter 7

Page 67, line 5: *Prisoners Without Trial*, p. 75.

Page 74, line 6: Rechs Ann Pedersen. "Return of the Evacuees." Santa Cruz Public Libraries. 12 March 2006. http://www.santacruzpl.org/history/ww2/9066/return.shtml

Page 75, line 6: Merle Miller. *Plain Speaking: An Oral Biography of Harry S. Truman.* New York: Berkley Publishing Company, 1974, pp. 452–453.

Page 75, line 19: *By Order of the President*, p. 258.

Chapter 8

Page 78, line 4: Stephen Magagnini. "A Nation's Apology: Formal Gesture Erases a Half Century of Shame." 8 Oct. 2001. 8 March 2006. www.sacbee.com/static/archive/news/projects/reparations/20011008_main.html

Page 78, line 25: Gerald R. Ford. "Proclamation 4417, Confirming the Termination of the Executive Order Authorizing Japanese American Internment During World War II." 19 Feb. 1976. Gerald R. Ford Library and Museum. 10 March 2006. www.ford.utexas.edu/LIBRARY/speeches/760111p.htm

Page 79, lines 9 and 13: *Justice Delayed*, p. 106.

Page 80, line 6: Ibid., p. 114.

Page 81, line 12: Ibid., pp. 173–174.

Page 82, line 3: Ibid., p. 243.

Page 82, line 8: "A Nation's Apology: Formal Gesture Erases a Half Century of Shame."

Select Bibliography

Burton, Jeffrey F., et al. *Confinement and Ethnicity: An Overview of World War II Japanese American Relocation Sites.* Seattle: University of Washington Press, 2002.

Dallek, Robert. *Franklin D. Roosevelt and American Foreign Policy, 1932–1945.* New York: Oxford University Press, 1979.

Daniels, Roger. *Prisoners Without Trial: Japanese Americans in World War II.* Rev. ed. New York: Hill and Wang, 2004.

Hansen, Arthur A., ed. *Japanese American World War II Evacuation Oral History Project. Part IV: Resisters.* Munich, Germany: K.G. Saur, 1995.

Irons, Peter, ed. *Justice Delayed: The Record of the Japanese American Internment Cases.* Middletown, Conn.: Wesleyan University Press, 1989.

Inada, Lawson Fusao, ed. *Only What We Could Carry: The Japanese American Internment Experience.* Berkeley, Calif.: Heyday Books, 2000.

Robinson, Greg. *By Order of the President: FDR and the Internment of Japanese Americans.* Cambridge, Mass.: Harvard University Press, 2001.

Further Reading

Collier, Christopher, and James Lincoln Collier. *The United States in World War II, 1941–1945.* New York: Benchmark Books, 2002.

Cooper, Michael. *Remembering Manzanar: Life in a Japanese Relocation Camp.* New York: Clarion Books, 2002.

Perl, Lila. *Behind Barbed Wire: The Story of Japanese American Internment During World War II.* New York: Benchmark Books, 2003.

Uchida, Yoshiko. *Desert Exile: The Uprooting of a Japanese American Family.* Seattle: University of Washington Press, 1982.

Wakatsuki, Jeanne Houston, and James Houston. *Farewell to Manzanar: A True Story of Japanese American Experience During and After the World War II Internment.* Boston: Houghton Mifflin, 2002.

Zurlo, Tony. *The Japanese Americans.* San Diego: Lucent Books, 2003.

Index

ABOUT THE AUTHOR

Michael Burgan is a freelance writer for both children and adults. A history graduate of the University of Connecticut, he has written more than 90 fiction and nonfiction books for children. He specializes in U.S. history. Michael has also written news articles, essays, and plays. He is a recipient of an Educational Press Association of America award.

IMAGE CREDITS